I0411636

Globalization has produced a new of level of interdependence among us. The economy and multinational supply chains do not abide by political boundaries. A computer ordered in Brazil is designed in California and assembled in several other countries. Economic integration was the first strong evidence of a new era.

Eduardo Paes

Growing up, my grandmother did not want worldly music in the house. Then when I went out to California, I started listening to Spanish music, mostly Mexican music. But were I in Egypt, I would listen to the music of the people, or if I was in Italy, I'd listen to Italian music.

Maya Angelou

We need Hawaii just as much and a good deal more than we did California. It is Manifest Destiny.

William McKinley

Crucial to understanding federalism in modern day America is the concept of mobility, or 'the ability to vote with your feet.' If you don't support the death penalty and citizens packing a pistol - don't come to Texas. If you don't like medicinal marijuana and gay marriage, don't move to

California.

Rick Perry

When I was eight, I would look at the cover of the 'Ghost Rider' comic book in my little home in Long Beach, California, and I couldn't get my head around how something that scary could also be good. To me it was my first philosophical awakening - 'How is this possible, this duality?'

Nicolas Cage

I was six months old at the time that I was taken, with my mother and father, from Sacramento, California, and placed in internment camps in the United States.

Robert Matsui

When I got out of coaching, I had taught a class at the University of California, an extension class on football for fans. I was looking for tools. I was showing them films. I was going to write a textbook. Trip Hawkins came to me about making it a game for computers.

John Madden

In California, there are huge problems because of dams. I'm against big dams, per se, because I think that they are economically unfeasible. They're ecologically unsustainable. And they're hugely undemocratic.

Arundhati Roy

There are not many places in the world where you can get to the beach in an hour, the desert in two hours and snowboarding or skiing in three hours. You can do all that in California.

Alex Pettyfer

I prefer to call the most obnoxious feminists what they really are: feminazis. Tom Hazlett, a good friend who is an esteemed and highly regarded professor of economics at the University of California at Davis, coined the term to describe any female who is intolerant of any point of view that challenges militant feminism.

Rush Limbaugh

The thing about Chicago is that it really isn't like any other place. The architecture and the layout of the city are the best. I'm from the Midwest, and consider myself a Midwesterner. I feel most at home there. I love California. I have great friends in California. I just have always considered Illinois to be home.

Vince Vaughn

In terms of mathematics textbooks, why can't you have the scale of a national market? Right now, we have a Texas textbook that's different from a California textbook that's different from a Massachusetts textbook. That's very expensive.

Bill Gates

There is science, logic, reason; there is thought verified by experience. And then there is California.

Edward Abbey

When I was a kid, I always wanted to live in California because I liked skateboarding.

Demetri Martin

This land is your land, this land is my land, From California to the New York Island. From the redwood forest to the Gulf Stream waters This land was made for you and me.

Woody Guthrie

I was going to go to a four-year college and be an anthropologist or to an art school and be an illustrator when a friend convinced me to learn photography at the University of Southern California. Little did I know it was a school that taught you how to make movies! It had never occurred to me that I'd ever have any interest in filmmaking.

George Lucas

My favorite drink is water - the bland one: Evian. I stick with that. I celebrate in the evening sometimes with Perrier. That's why I love coming to California. They're always talking to you about bottled water.

George Foreman

My parents separated before I was 1 year old. I moved in with my aunt and uncle when I was in fourth grade. I was, like, 8 or 9 years old. I was getting in a lot of trouble when I was in Southern California. My older sisters were in gangs. My older brother was in gangs.

Troy Polamalu

In Los Angeles all the loose objects in the country were collected, as if America had been tilted and everything that wasn't tightly screwed down had slid into Southern California.

Saul Bellow

My mother was a very wonderful woman. When she and my dad divorced, she moved to California and worked two jobs in the cannery at night and as a waitress during the day. But she saved enough money to establish a restaurant.

Dolores Huerta

We need to incorporate that age-old concept of redemption into the work that we do in the criminal justice system in California.

Kamala Harris

If you're the type of person who has to fulfill your dreams, you've gotta be resourceful to make sure you can do it. I came out to California when I was 21, thinking my New York credentials would take me all the way. I came back home a year later all dejected and a failure.

Vin Diesel

Object-oriented programming is an exceptionally bad idea which could only have originated in California.

Edsger Dijkstra

In any democratic, civilized - even non-democratic nations, if you are a nation, it means to say that in our case, if there's a hurricane in Louisiana, the people of Vermont are there for them. If there's a tornado in the Midwest, we are there for them. If there's flooding in the East Coast, the people in California are there for us.

Bernie Sanders

California is a fine place to live - if you happen to be an orange.

Fred Allen

Texas has done a very good job of securing their borders with the help of the federal government. California has done a good job.

Jan Brewer

I want to spend 100 percent of my time focused on what I think I can make the biggest difference on as the governor of California.

Meg Whitman

Regulation is strangling businesses of all sizes in California, and we've got to streamline regulation so it's easy, not hard, to do business.

Meg Whitman

I came at age in the '60s, and initially my hopes and dreams were invested in politics and the movements of the time - the anti-war movement, the civil rights movement. I worked on Bobby Kennedy's campaign for president as a teenager in California and the night he was killed.

David Talbot

Everything is just better in California - the wine, the food, fruits and vegetables, the comforts of living. Even the instrumentalists are generous and curious. Everything is wonderful.

Beth Anderson

I was born and raised in Santa Cruz, California, and the whole lifestyle revolves around the beach. My parents met surfing, and the beach was a major part of our daily lives.

Marisa Miller

I was born and raised in California and benefited from California's excellent public schools, from kindergarten through medical school.

Ami Bera

Twice the Republicans in the California legislature tried to block my seating because of my trips to Hanoi.

Tom Hayden

But the most important thing is, Enron did not cause the California crisis.

Kenneth Lay

The California I knew, old rancho California, is gone. It just doesn't exist, except maybe in little pockets. I lived on the edge of the Mojave Desert, an area that used to be farm country. There were all these fresh-produce stands with avocados and date palms. You could get a dozen artichokes for a buck or something. Totally wiped out now.

Sam Shepard

My mother Elizabeth Ivey Brubeck was a pianist who studied with Dame Myra Hess and Tobias Matthey. As a child in California I used to listen to her play Chopin.

Dave Brubeck

For me, I love California. I feel like it's my second home in that I moved out by choice at eighteen. It gave me opportunities that I didn't have anywhere else.

Vince Vaughn

Well, California used to be in the dream-making business, and unfortunately what's happened I think we're now in the dream-breaking business.

Meg Whitman

When I was still in high school I knew I wanted to live in California.

Tila Tequila

I must confess, I'm not the best cook. I make a mean salsa, as I like hot sauce and, you know, tacos, because I'm a California kid, and that's about it.

Sasha Grey

How would Elvira run the state of California? Well, there isn't much I could do that is worse than what Arnold Schwarzenegger has done. Running it into the damn ground. If I was running the whole nation? I would have free Netflix movies for everyone.

Cassandra Peterson

I finally had to go to the American Civil Liberties Union here in northern California to get my reply published to what I considered to be a hatchet job done by Stanley Crouch.

Ishmael Reed

In California, we have some of the strongest consumer protection laws in the country. While it is easy to conceive of innovation and regulation as mutually exclusive, California is proof that we can do both. We can innovate responsibly.

Kamala Harris

You know, I think, people of all stripes in California, Republicans, Democrats, conservatives, liberals, frankly, as I have traveled the state, the number one issue is jobs. And they are looking for which candidate can get the economy back on track.

Meg Whitman

When I moved out here to California, I became obsessed with geology. It's impossible not to be interested in the earth if you live in a place like this. I started to read a lot of geology, much to the horror of my friends.

Jamaica Kincaid

Already this war on gangs in California is taking money from universities to build prisons, and the universities have some clout.

Tom Hayden

Certainly being in California has encouraged a sustained commitment to rethinking the nature, purposes, and relevance of the contemporary arts, specifically music, for a society which by and large seems to manage quite well without them.

Brian Ferneyhough

I mean, I'm humble... to me, I'm just a regular cat from Oakland, California.

Lance Gross

My father was second-generation Chinese-American, born in 1923 in California. My mother emigrated to the States from China when she was in her early twenties, in part to escape the political turmoil in China.

Tess Gerritsen

When Proposition 8 passed in California, some were quick to blame minority voters, some of whom had voted for both President Obama and Proposition 8; however, these claims were later debunked as being overstated.

Christine Pelosi

My career in racing started at a very young age in California.

Jeff Gordon

Mazomanie doesn't even have a stoplight, so it doesn't do a lot. But the cheese curds there are unbelievable. I've never had them anywhere else, even at places in California that claim to have the real thing. There's a cheese factory in Arena, Mazomanie's neighboring town, and they'll give you fresh curds that are so amazing.

Skylar Grey

I always got a kick out of it when they called it the California Sound because it really came out of Liverpool and Greenwich Village.

Roger McGuinn

With my ministry of light, part of what I do is work on the California Alliance For Arts Education.

Sally Kirkland

My favorite drive is Highway 101 in California between Los Angeles and San Luis Obispo. I love the 101; Highway 1 is too windy, and 5 is too boring - the 101 is just right. It's like the Mama Bear of scenic drives.

Art Alexakis

California is a place of invention, a place of courage, a place of vision, a place of the future. People who made California what it is were willing to take risks, think outside convention and build.

Nicolas Berggruen

I like being a foreigner. For me, to live in California is very pleasant - I'm more comfortable not feeling a part of everything, not feeling responsible for the government or the roads or the health system.

Eric Idle

California is lucky, the East Coast is lucky because we get great seafood and a lot of produce from Florida, locally in good weather, but in the winter we have to buy it.

Eric Ripert

The completion of my undergraduate training at the University of California (Berkeley) provided just the needed touches of rigor at advanced levels in both economics and mathematics.

Lawrence R. Klein

It's ludicrous that my friends in California aren't able to legally get married. It's a civil rights issue. In 20 years we're going to look back at tapes of these antigay people saying ridiculous things on the news and it's going to sound as antiquated as the newsreels of horrible racists from the '50s.

Busy Philipps

The thing that really surprised me about strip malls in California, specifically Los Angeles, is that they have some really fantastic restaurants.

Dave Foley

Well, I'll tell you, one of things I'm proud of is for someone from Southern California, who didn't grow up around coal mines, I learned a lot that tragic day we lost twenty-nine miners at Upper Big Branch coal mine.

Hilda Solis

While I'm in L.A. I always make time for my favorite activity which is hiking. The trails in California are amazing, as they are always challenging, and I never get bored from all the beautiful scenery.

Dylan Lauren

I was raised with the Bible Belt mentality, and by coming to California, I came out of this dark place and unlearned a lot of things I'd been taught.

Edward Ruscha

I've been in California for about 15 years now. You're always in your car and insulated. I miss New York so much.

Jimmy Smits

For years I drove a big Ford F250 pickup. That was my ride because two-thirds of my work was wood work, and I'm always driving up to Northern California, where I harvest salvaged trees.

Nick Offerman

It's a coup by the GOP to grab the governorship to California to make this place a safe haven for George W.

Bush in 2004. It's incredible when you think about it. The recall cost the state $100 million.

Al Jardine

You know, we - if, for example, Jerry Brown can withstand, you know, what will probably end up being $200 million of spending by his opponent and get elected governor of California, that will be a big victory in the nation's largest state.

David Axelrod

When I finish as the host of 'Jeopardy!' I'm going to go up to Taft in central California. They have a small college there that teaches you about oil drilling.

Alex Trebek

I answer that question by saying: 'Why Meg Whitman' which is: I'm not a career politician. I spent 30 years in business. I can tell you that people in California have had it with career politicians: they are done.

Meg Whitman

I want to work with the teachers' union. But as I said out there, we have to put the kids first and we are letting down a generation of California children. It's not acceptable.

Meg Whitman

I'm not a career politician. I spent 30 years in business. I can tell you that people in California have had it with career politicians: they are done.

Meg Whitman

This line of research continued when I went, and brought my research group with me, to the new University of California, Irvine campus in 1966 to become the founding Dean of the School of Physical Sciences.

Frederick Reines

Four hours of prosthetics every morning, the jowls and the nose, and it was very hot so they're having to attend to it all day, and you're still petrified of so many things, such as, can I speak properly? Hitchcock never quite lost those East End vowels, even though he had the softened California consonants.

Toby Jones

It's funny, but when I arrived in California to start college I was much more interested in becoming a surfer and cruise along in life from one beach to the next. I didn't plan out any huge career for myself.

Benicio Del Toro

Even though I grew up surfing and sailing in Southern California, I was born horse crazy.

Bo Derek

I will embrace the first opportunity to get to California and it is altogether probable that when once there I shall never again leave it.

George Stoneman

California has something which not every place in the world has: It has what I would call a sunny side, and I don't mean just physically, but the sunny side is a future. California's worth saving, to put it bluntly.

Nicolas Berggruen

Battering down solar cells on the roofs of Wal-Marts in California. I think that will be some of the highest-return investments that anyone ever makes.

Jeremy Grantham

The increase in inequality in income is a longtime trend, but the pressure on middle- and low-income workers is going up rapidly. Especially if they live in an area where there are high housing and gas prices, like California.

Alice Rivlin

As someone who has grown up living in Southern California, I know all too well about the costs and scarcities of water.

Ed Begley, Jr.

The first two pictures I did, I played a young student in prep school. When I did Lifeguard, everyone was saying, You're so Southern California. It was a surprise to me.

Parker Stevenson

My record at the University of California as an

undergraduate was mediocre to say the best.

Douglass North

I'm pursuing soundtrack work in the southern California
area and down the line I plan to make a moody, intense
acoustic album. Not all acoustic, but an acoustic - oriented
guitar record that I've already written most of the material
for.

Ronnie Montrose

It was clear that the special interest groups in California
really wanted the Chinese to be shut out of the country,
because that was where the racial tension was the greatest.

Iris Chang

If you're a kid in Southern California, somebody - whether
it's you or your parents - somebody throws your hat into the
ring and I think everyone had a commercial or two.

Danny Bonaduce

As governor of California in 1970, Reagan endeared
himself to millions of conservatives nationwide when he

publicly rebuked the anti-war movement that was exploding on college campuses.

Jackson Katz

I love California. It has such a strong contribution to the history of culture, and popular culture. For better and worse, of course. Even the worst can be interesting to some degree sometimes for somebody creative.

Hedi Slimane

There have been some good studies done in California with Hispanic parents where in the course of a year, they have changed their entire nutritional intake for the better. The kid becomes, in a sense, the bridge between the educational process and the home.

C. Everett Koop

I've been through the process qualifying for the World Cup, which is an amazing, two-year process. It was an honor to represent the U.S. and to represent the city of Los Angeles and California.

Cobi Jones

It was jarring to be berated for 'acting white' when I was placed in a predominantly black middle school in Southern California. I was also chubby, into boys who weren't into me, and tried too hard to fit into this 'blackness' I was supposed to be.

Issa Rae

Iranians call California and Iran 'sister cities;' they're very much alike. Iranians feel at home here and the weather is so close to Iranian weather.

Shohreh Aghdashloo

I'm very stodgy. I'm always looking at old photos of California and Los Angeles, knowing that what I'm looking at is now full of houses. There used to be vacant lots in Los Angeles, now all taken up by three-storey boxes - it's all getting infilled.

Edward Ruscha

I like loud music. I like music that fills my ears. I'm just going to pull out my iPod and see what we got here. We're always interested in new bands because we have a retail store in northern California. I think it's got to be happy.

Tyler Florence

When we acquired California and New- Mexico this party, scorning all compromises and all concessions, demanded that slavery should be forever excluded from them, and all other acquisitions of the Republic, either by purchase or conquest, forever.

Robert Toombs

I did my undergraduate work at the University of California when it was still affordable. But tuition keeps on rising.

Joseph DeRisi

If there was any other place I would live, other than Miami, it would be California. It's beautiful. The weather is just gorgeous, I love being here, too.

Jon Secada

Where gays and lesbians are the best organized and most concentrated in numbers are states that President Clinton must carry in order to be reelected in 1996. Among the states are California, New York, Michigan, Oregon, Washington, Massachusetts, Illinois.

David Mixner

My father was a small-town banker. He became very ill when I was 10 years old, and we went to California three years later in an attempt to recover his health, which never happened.

Warren Christopher

I'm a California girl, right? I grew up with that farm-to-table dining before it was sweeping the nation.

Meghan Markle

I know who I am as an artist and I know what my sound is, but I wanted to know what I could do in order to take it to that next level. So the experiences I had last year of moving to California and traveling to places like Rome and Nicaragua where I met a lot of people just had a really big impact in my life.

Kate Voegele

While it may be difficult to understand why cities and even entire states would doom themselves to insolvency by undertaking these obligations, the answer is simple: Democratic politicians, who have near-total political control of California and of America's biggest cities, support this massive transfer of wealth to public employees.

Devin Nunes

Over the years, I've traveled to many places for inspiration and research, including Pennsylvania, Ohio, South Carolina, California, and Hawaii.

Jennifer Chiaverini

It's exciting for me to be home in California where I'm from and to be working with Victoria's Secret.

Lindsay Ellingson

In 1979, I received a phone call from Ansel Adams asking me if I would be willing to consider coming to work for him. I was teaching photography in Southern California at that point.

John Sexton

When I was in the California legislature in the '80s, the organic growers, who were sort of the small hippie farmers in those days, brought it to my attention that there were no regulations on organic labeling. In essence, anybody could just grow a thing any way they wanted and put 'organic' on it.

Sam Farr

On my recent trip to the Mexico border, Border Patrol agents in California told me they have arrested the same coyotes 20 times, but they are not prosecuted.

Ric Keller

So that was Reagan's political problem. As a rancher in California, he was an environmentalist himself. But the President of the United States doesn't control everything that happens in Washington.

Brian Mulroney

I always enjoyed art history because, growing up in California, my exposure was limited, and it was a new experience. To learn the history of art opened up certain things to me, made me see. It intrigued me.

Herb Ritts

What I particularly liked was that, coming from California and not being involved in the New York scene, I developed my personal way, in my own way, at my own pace.

Herb Ritts

I know there are lots of regional accents in England, but I can't tell them apart and I'm not really aware of class. I don't pay any attention to those boundaries. I'm a California girl.

Danielle de Niese

This union has been divided in like a civil war - brother against brother - sister against sister. And I'm pulling it together. We've already seen evidence of that in New York, in Pennsylvania, in California. The first thing is we have to get on the same page. We have to be united in one cause.

James P. Hoffa

My most memorable teacher was Rich Campe, my third-grade teacher at Fairlands Elementary in Pleasanton, California.

Deb Caletti

In California, there is a strong tension between north and south.

Thomas Mars

My father was a member of the Teamsters Union in California, where he helped to organize better health care for workers. My mother worked for more than 20 years on an assembly line.

Hilda Solis

I am presently in my thirteenth year of teaching a graduate course at the University of Southern California.

Shelley Berman

California has the highest number of illegal immigrants residing in its borders. The estimated number of illegal alien residents in California was about 2.2 million, or nearly 32 percent of the total number of illegal immigrants in the United States.

Gary Miller

The great medley of Oregon and California emigrants, at

their camps around Independence, had heard reports that several additional parties were on the point of setting out from St. Joseph's farther to the northward.

Francis Parkman

Sometimes I think I might not have written 'The Age of Miracles' if I hadn't grown up in California, if I hadn't been exposed to its very particular blend of beauty and disaster, of danger and denial.

Karen Thompson Walker

I'm such a tomboy - I was raised in the South - and I also really wanted to work in New York, being so different from California, though it was a freezing-cold winter.

Jessica Stroup

Fences would be a hindrance to terrorists should they decide to come across a land border between the U.S. and Mexico and to California.

Duncan Hunter

When I first heard Ray Charles, he was a flop artist on a

small label in California. He hadn't sold any records. And I bought his contract for $2,500.

Ahmet Ertegun

Let me share some facts with you about the law in most of our country. California is in many ways a little different from the rest of the world, and California has better gun laws than many states, although California's need to be improved.

Michael D. Barnes

I came from a really musical family. I studied classical piano because my grandparents were piano teachers, but started doing musical theater at age nine in Fresno, California, and went to a performing arts high school. That was my life.

Audra McDonald

I've lived in California for six years and I've never surfed.

Bill Skarsgard

All the clothes in my closet are Oakland, California,

clothes. You can't wear those anywhere else. The barometric pressure drops and then where are you?

Mary Roach

I am most grateful for having bad eyesight, which prevented me from becoming a commercial pilot and instead, led me to having the best job in the world - representing the people of California's 47th Congressional District.

Loretta Sanchez

California must be all American or all Chinese. We are resolved that it shall be American, and are prepared to make it so. May we not rely upon your sympathy and assistance?

Denis Kearney

I know there's a great deal that Arnold Schwarzenegger could teach me about making movies. There's a great deal I could teach him about the fiscal reforms that are needed - desperately needed - to set California back in good order.

Tom McClintock

My uncle who helped in a big part of raising me from when I was young, had moved from California, and would just tell me these legendary stories of these motorcycle clubs that he was around and that he used to ride with.

Theo Rossi

Portland is a really great city, especially because I'm a shopper and there's no sales tax! That really adds up so fast, because in California, a $1000 pair of shoes ends up costing another $100.

Bitsie Tulloch

California has set up regional collection offices around the world, staffed by California employees, specifically for out of state California businesses to collect the money and bring it back to California.

Craig Benson

People began to understand that with the acquisition of California the nation had obtained practically half a continent, of which the future possibilities were almost unlimited, so far as the development of natural resources and the genera production of wealth were concerned.

John Moody

The construction of extensive railways, however, and particularly the consolidation of small, experimental lines into large systems, dates from the days of the discovery of gold in California.

John Moody

I think the executives have matured enough so that they recognize that we have a two-party system. In California, we have more than a two-party system.

Lew Wasserman

I was born and raised in Huntington Beach, California. I was very athletic, playing volleyball and softball. I did gymnastics for about ten years, too.

Jasmine Tookes

I was raised on technology. I grew up in Livermore, California, a town of physicists and cowboys. My parents worked at the government laboratories there. So technology was very normal for me.

Cynthia Breazeal

I love Disneyland because the teacups are so awesome. But California Adventure is the best.

Joey King

I'm a free market person, a free trader. But if we had a market in California, there would be competition.

Anna Eshoo

I think Yandex is something in between two different cultures. One originated from the old Soviet culture of the scientific institute. It was a free atmosphere of scientists, maybe too free because nobody cared about making money. Another origin is something close to what you usually see in California startups.

Arkady Volozh

Bobby and I have been to various reunions of Our Gang. We've been to like three or four reunions over the past 15 years or so. We were at one in Palm Springs, California.

Tommy Bond

Here in California, it's living the life, going to school, playing sports and hanging out with my friends. But, when I'm in North Carolina, its all work, work, work.

Jackson Brundage

I had the pleasure of knowing Ronald Reagan before he became Governor of California. He was a truly great human being and we usually spent our time together reminiscing about mutual friends.

James Arness

California is an island, and New York's an island. Maybe it's time for me to change islands.

Paul Mazursky

There was a time I wouldn't fly to California if I had to spend the night. Can you believe it? I would not fly to California, the phrase was, 'if the sun has to set on me.' I just had prejudices against it.

John Cullum

My family actually owns an MMA promotion company, so

it's kind of a family deal. It's called Fight Sports Entertainment, and they throw amateur fights in California. Because of that, I've given my mom a lot of the fighters to fight in a show.

Jonathan Lipnicki

I support an assault weapons ban, and I'll tell you why. We already have one in California, so I don't support doing anything above what we do in California.

Eric Swalwell

One of my goals here in Congress, being the youngest member of the California delegation, is to really try and get the institution to upgrade the way it communicates with its constituents.

Eric Swalwell

I live on the beautiful Northern California coast. I have always loved hiking, whale watching and being outdoors.

Christine Feehan

My dad wanted me to be a professional person, which I was

- I was a civil engineer. I graduated from civil engineering at USC in California. I became an engineer, and I helped design the roads for the L.A. County Roads Department. And I did that for about one and a half years in a sense to please my parents - to be a 'respectable' person.

James Hong

I've been telling people 'I'm going to go to California, and I'm going to be a big star' since the womb, but lately it was immediately followed by, 'Would you like soup or salad with that?'

Diane Ruggiero

When I first came to California, it was fun and exciting to get any part in any movie and get paid for it. Because of my size and my background, it seemed like I was right for just about anything.

Kevin Peter Hall

I live in Hollywood, California. It's absolutely nothing like Absaroka County, Wyoming. For me, it's a great escape and I really enjoy it.

Bailey Chase

I won the youth vote in Massachusetts and in California. I did very well with it in Ohio.

Hillary Clinton

The longest, most solid and complex relationship in my life is with my mother. It started before I was born, and now, when I am 71 and living in California and she is 92 and living in Chile, we are still in touch daily.

Isabel Allende

California is going to take themselves off the cliff culturally and economically, fiscally. They are going to be at the trough in Washington wanting a bailout.

Jim DeMint

It shone on everyone, whether they had a contract or not. The most democratic thing I'd ever seen, that California sunshine.

Angela Carter

The studio scene in California is sort of ridiculous anyway.

Paul Kantner

One thing that improved my cooking skills was being a poor student in California... If you don't have much money, you have to learn to cook.

Diane Mott Davidson

You could have a hit in California that no one had heard of in Oklahoma.

Wanda Jackson

As a young surgeon in training at the University of California San Francisco General Hospital in the early '80s, my colleagues and I were inundated with an epidemic of young men with fevers, rashes, swollen lymph nodes and eventually death.

Richard Carmona

I hope it will be set in California. In a way, I made a mistake, because a New Jersey policeman can't operate that way in New York. But in California, he can move between different counties.

Patricia Highsmith

By means of steam one can go from California to Japan in eighteen days.

Townsend Harris

My graduate studies were carried out at the California Institute of Technology.

Kenneth G. Wilson

I live in one of the coastal cities in Southern California, and every so often I like to take a walk down the boardwalk in Venice during the weekends when it is abuzz with lively activity.

Al Seckel

It is clear that a temporary increase in the cap is needed to ensure high-tech companies can hire the specialized personnel they need to continue to help fuel California's economic growth.

Pete Wilson

I'm not really a Hollywood person. Not that I don't like L.A., but I'm just a Northern California guy.

Clint Eastwood

I was born in Sherman Oaks, California.

Jennifer Aniston

Growing up as a kid, we moved all over the country on a fairly frequent basis, from New Jersey to Texas, California, Illinois... we moved 21 times in my first 17 years.

J. Michael Straczynski

I didn't study writing. I didn't write anything substantial until I got to California.

Joss Whedon

California, in a sense, is almost Starbucks' largest country, with almost 3,000 stores.

Howard Schultz

It's a tough problem that a company faces once they branch out beyond one set of offices in California into that big bad world out there.

Rebecca MacKinnon

I'm happy wherever I go, whatever I do. I'm happy in Iowa, I'm happy here in California.

Ashton Kutcher

Obviously the Senate is a federal office, but to get California's economy moving again we need to do some things in the federal arena.

Carly Fiorina

There are Tea Parties, and I would say plural, in California.

Carly Fiorina

California is beautiful to look at, but you can't be a part of it like you can in Michigan.

Jennifer Granholm

Not much about California, on its own preferred terms, has encouraged its children to see themselves as connected to one another.

Joan Didion

I'm never going to get married again. Three strikes, you're out. I think if I would try to get married again in California, I have to go to prison, don't I? I think you only get three.

Roseanne Barr

Although I'm living in California, I'm very proud to be British.

Rod Stewart

Helsinki may not be as cold as you make it out to be, but California is still a lot nicer. I don't remember the last time I couldn't walk around in shorts all day.

Linus Torvalds

In California, up to 15 percent of wells in agricultural areas exceed a federal contaminant threshold, according to studies.

Charles Duhigg

If we could do high-speed rail in California just half a notch above what they've done on the Shanghai line in China, and if we had a straight path from L.A. to San Francisco, as well as the milk run, at least that would be progress.

Elon Musk

But ours was intended to be a citizen government. It is what of, by and for the people means. And when our most important issue in California is the creation of jobs, I think it's quite helpful to have someone in the U.S. Senate or in the governor's seat who actually knows where jobs come from.

Carly Fiorina

Well, first, if I am fortunate enough to be elected to the U.S. Senate, it won't be a party that will have elected me. It will be the people of California.

Carly Fiorina

For some reason and I don't know why, but I don't think

that I'm funny in California. So I always want to do my movies east somewhere.

Kevin James

It's a shame about California, and particularly about L.A., where they've demolished so many landmarks. It's a bit of a disease there, where if anything is over 30 years old, they sort of knock it down and replace it. It's a strange town, it's this sprawling suburb, and then there's a city, the old town.

Gary Oldman

I said we are going to balance an $11 billion budget deficit in a $29 billion budget, so by percentage, the largest budget deficit in America, by percentage, larger than California, larger than New York, larger than Illinois. And we're going to balance that without raising taxes on the people of the state of New Jersey.

Chris Christie

After my parents' divorce when I was 4, I spent weekends with my dad before we finally moved to California. By the time Sunday rolled around, I was incapable of enjoying the day's activities, of being in the moment, because I was already dreading the inevitable goodbye of Sunday evening.

Rob Lowe

I'm thankful for Sarah Palin's vice presidential bid, which taught us that Alaska is not in a box off the coast of California.

Paula Poundstone

I grew up in the Midwest, quite far from any ocean or any beach, a million miles. I think for kids who grew up where I did, the idea of California, surfing and beach life was so exotic and glamorous.

John Malkovich

I lead a very conventional life. I don't lead a writer's life. And I think that can be a source of suspicion and irritation to some people. This was more true when I was living in California, when I didn't lead a writer's life at all.

Joan Didion

The Democratic Party of California is ready to sponsor me. All I have to do is find the right office to run for.

Bobby Darin

I was born and raised in Queens and moved into the city as a young adult. Then I ended up acting and decided to run off to California.

Debi Mazar

I graduated from the University of California, Los Angeles, with an English literature degree and travelled for a year before going to work.

Natalie Massenet

I've enjoyed my time in the American League, the fans of Southern California and other friendships.

Joe Torre

I experienced the California Northridge Earthquake of 1994 and the eruption of Mount St. Helens in 1980, and I have thus seen firsthand how terrible and awesomely devastating a force of nature can be.

Paul Watson

You always read stories of people going out to California

and making it as an actor with, like, two dollars, so I figured I'd try it.

Adam Driver

I moved to New York from California when I was 11, so initially I was seen as the California person for a while. I didn't feel like I was popular, but I did feel confident.

Gwyneth Paltrow

I want to caucus in Iowa. I'll caucus all over the state. I don't caucus in California. You don't caucus where you live. It doesn't look good.

Pat Paulsen

I believe in that old adage that 'as goes California, so goes the country.'

Kamala Harris

I move between San Francisco and Paris... I have a wonderful beach house in California.

Danielle Steel

I'm the worst surfer in California. My balance is off from boxing.

Mickey Rourke

'King of California' was just, I thought, a really great, fresh, original kind of script. I loved the tone, the mix of tragedy, comedy, and drama, and that it was a good part.

Michael Douglas

There are still states that have not evolved so much as California, that still skimp on recognition and, even worse, the rights of immigrants.

Enrique Pena Nieto

I think the best restaurants in America should be in California.

David Chang

I opened a restaurant that had nothing but California wines.

Paul Prudhomme

California is responsible for selling, trading and distributing large amounts of shark fins that come from all over the world.

Ted Danson

I went to college for about a year in California.

Seann William Scott

My family owns a music store in Claremont, California, called The Claremont Folk Music Center.

Ben Harper

Just as Bowie, Zeppelin, etc., became rock stars by remaking themselves in the image of the California girls, the Go-Gos became rock stars by pretending to be the Buzzcocks and the Sex Pistols. Jane Wiedlin always said her biggest influence was growing up in L.A. as a Bowie girl.

Rob Sheffield

The records of adopted children are sealed in California.

That seal is considered inviolable... The judge ruled that, because I was famous, he didn't have the same rights as other kids.

Danielle Steel

The four places I've called home in my life have been Lahore, London, New York and California. And I have a very strong tie to each one of those four places.

Mohsin Hamid

He was doing - Ray was designing the clothes for my mom's show from California. And one of the first appearances I ever made on television was on my mother's show and Ray and Bob did the clothes for that. It has been a long time.

Liza Minnelli

Ah, the bond between English boys and California girls. For those of us who aren't either, it's a bond that fascinates and mystifies. So much of the world's favorite music comes out of that relationship.

Rob Sheffield

Concord, California was a great place to grow up.

Dave Brubeck

My own Brubeck Institute in California is turning out fantastic young jazz players, and I know great things will happen.

Dave Brubeck

When I made 'Who Needs Pictures,' my first album, I had been west of the Mississippi River one time in my life, and that was in fourth grade. We traveled to California for vacation and stayed with some friends of my parents. It was culture shock, and it was different.

Brad Paisley

I've always wanted to be able to say that I come from Los Angeles, California and feel quintessentially American - even if I said that in Spanish.

Cheech Marin

The oil dinosaurs want to win so badly in my home state because what happens here matters everywhere. The nation often follows where California goes.

Rebecca Solnit

I first saw the ocean as a kid. We would drive from Arizona in the summer and arrive as the sun was starting to come down over the hill near Laguna in southern California. We would always sing a song, and it was a big joyous family moment when we came over the hill.

Ted Danson

I arrived in California with no job, no car, and no money, but, like millions of other girls, a dream.

Victoria Principal

But the truth is, growing up in California, we knew nothing about hockey.

Leigh Steinberg

Death Valley is really wide-open - it's bigger than Rhode Island - and it's less a part of California than an ungoverned territory, so there's lots of weird cops-and-robbers stuff going on.

Gus Van Sant

When I got traded to the California Angels, I really wasn't that excited about going to the Angels because it meant changing leagues and also a whole new set of teammates. But shortly after I got there I realized that it was one of the best things that ever happened to me.

Nolan Ryan

Before I lived in America, my husband and I did a Californian road trip. We took a month, starting off in L.A. I love the landscapes of California: one moment you're in the desert, the next you're up in the Napa Valley or by the water in Big Bear.

Ashley Jensen

We never work on only one project because we never know if we will get permission for a project. So, for 'Over the River,' we started in 1992. I was just finishing 'The Umbrellas' in Japan and California, and I was also working on getting permission to wrap the Reichstag.

Christo

L.A. prides itself on newness or being the last frontier or just not liking old things and tearing them down to build new things. But Malibu history is interesting to me. My mom's family was one of the early families in California, so there's history going back to the 1840s or '50s.

Kim Gordon

I am a California girl, born and raised, so flip-flops and cutoff shorts are my go-to look. An easy Angeleno uniform, so to speak. But for my role on 'Suits,' I'm dressed in Alexander McQueen, Tom Ford, and Prada almost every day. And therein lies the difference. For work, I wear art; in real life, I wear clothes.

Meghan Markle

That's an economic development program in the metropolitan area. If they don't see that, and you don't get these things done, then you're competing with Texas and California and Atlanta; then you really have problems.

Richard M. Daley

It never occurred to me that I could live in California. Now I can't imagine living anywhere else.

George Cukor

I love clothes! I shop everywhere, but I like Urban Outfitters, Forever 21, Nordstrom, and Neiman Marcus. It's a wide range. I'm from California, and I love the Pasadena Flea Market.

Keke Palmer

I live in Santa Fe, New Mexico. And I travel a tremendous amount. I'm in New York and California a lot, but then also I like faraway places a lot.

Ali MacGraw

My dad worked as an executive at Lockheed Aircraft and worked on the U-2 and things like that. My mother was a homemaker, and she was vice-president of the Democratic Council of California back in the '50s.

Robert Englund

Obviously California is fantastic in terms of produce, vegetables.

Eric Ripert

But indeed a market like California is not good for Enron.

Kenneth Lay

The problems in California have been that it's been very difficult to site and build new power plants.

Kenneth Lay

After the falling out with my father, I worked on a couple of ranches - thoroughbred layup farms, actually - out toward Chino, California. That was fine for a little while, but I wanted to get out completely, and twenty miles away wasn't far enough.

Sam Shepard

After I left Texas and went to California, I had a hard time getting anyone to play anything that I was writing, so I had to end up playing them myself. And that's how I ended up just being a saxophone player.

Ornette Coleman

We agreed that we cannot let personal political attacks get in the way of doing the very best we can for California's children.

Rob Reiner

When California provides the same value as other locations, I'd gladly shoot all my pictures here.

Joel Silver

I wrote all the lyrics on 'Good Vibrations' and most of them in 'Kokomo.' 'Kokomo' was extremely popular and fun to sing - it's probably one of the bigger sing-along songs in our show. But then 'Help Me Rhonda,' 'Surfin' USA' and 'California Girls' and 'I Get Around' and 'Fun, Fun, Fun' are great songs as well.

Mike Love

I enjoyed being in California for a while. But that's the thing about London: you can't really shake it. I've always had the impression when I was in L.A. for long periods of time that simultaneously my life was happening somewhere else, and I'm missing it.

Chiwetel Ejiofor

After the Second World War, I returned to California to study composition with Darius Milhaud, who wrote wonderful works like 'Le Boeuf sur le Toit' and 'La Cretion du Monde.' I especially enjoy his work for two pianos, 'Scaramouche.'

Dave Brubeck

If California ever developed a vineyard rating system, Saxum's James Berry Vineyard would be classified as one of the best.

Robert M. Parker, Jr.

Growing up in Southern California, it's all car culture. When I was a kid, I knew every single model of every single car dealer; I knew every style of every year.

Cheech Marin

Several unions have agreed to larger employee contributions for their members. Taxpayers are living with cuts and making sacrifices to deal with the reality of California's budget crisis, state workers are going to have to do the same.

Jerry Brown

Britain, and my hometown, will always be with me wherever I go and whatever I do - but I prefer to live in California.

Eric Burdon

And I want to be able to - you know, make Republicans and Democrats famous for keeping jobs in California.

Meg Whitman

I moved here to California when I was 13 to pursue my acting career.

Christina Milian

Living in Maryland, I saw that the opportunities were far greater in California than back home.

Christina Milian

I grew up in Boston, so it's a nice change to be cold after living in California.

Matt LeBlanc

One thing they don't have out here in California is Rita's Italian Ices. We used to have one right next to our house and it was so good!

Joe Jonas

I have two houses in California, and they're both within a couple of minutes from the beach. So, I definitely feel at home in California and by the ocean.

Marisa Miller

I'm from Santa Cruz in Northern California, and the 49ers were my dad and I's bonding time. We would go to games in the '80s. It was a good time to fall in love with football when your team was unstoppable.

Marisa Miller

I travelled to California when I was 18 and went to Los Angeles State College.

Robert Vaughn

My family didn't have any money growing up. I'm just a

girl from the ghetto; from Indio, California.

Vanessa Marcil

I always tell people I romanticize about doing something simple, like doing radio in northern California.

Craig Kilborn

I'm in California a lot; I go overseas sometimes and I meet more Hells Angels than other Angels do.

Chuck Zito

I think we can be the very best place to start a business, to grow a business, to invent a new technology, to change the world, to change the country. But we've got a lot of work to deliver a new California to the people of California.

Meg Whitman

We lose our right to be surprised that California has the highest recidivism rate in the country if we refuse to hire folks who have taken responsibility for their crimes and have done their time.

Greg Boyle

I do California casual a little bit better than really small European cut, tight apparel But I can rock some Gucci when I need to. I say this as I'm wearing Adidas sweatpants and a ten-year-old Chrome Hearts T-shirt.

Carson Daly

In California, especially Northern California, the fans really cheer for me.

Jeff Gordon

When I ask the young people from California why they want to go to New York, and the ones from the East why they're determined to go West, I hear what you'd expect: new challenges, different weather, boyfriends, girlfriends, to make a name... They laugh when I say, 'But your poor mother.'

Susan Estrich

I was introduced to the world of modern food production in the mid-1990s, while researching an article about California's strawberry industry for the 'Atlantic Monthly.'

Eric Schlosser

We've tried to get as much supply into California as we can.

Kenneth Lay

As a fluke, my great-grandfather hit one of the largest oil reserves in California.

Armie Hammer

I never really felt like I belonged in California.

Molly Ringwald

When this genre of music started in America, Metallica was up north in California, we were in Southern California, Anthrax was on the East Coast. We each developed our own metal music, and after 30 years, we're still playing our metal music.

Tom Araya

I have a really good band, and just returned from a short tour in California. It hasn't always gone that well.

Mick Taylor

I'm from California, and still live in LA.

Teena Marie

Instead of putting Americans to work, the Teamsters have been busy yanking members off projects and idling construction projects from California to Indiana to New York in order to shake down employers.

Michelle Malkin

One of the first things a British visitor to Southern California discovers is that he must have a car. Freeways. Bad public transport. I took driving lessons.

Christopher Lee

My friends tell me I'm the most boring celebrity they know! A typical night for me is at home in California or watching movies in my pyjamas.

Amber Riley

I like California a lot more than New York these days.

Dee Dee Ramone

I grew up in San Francisco in the 1970s. We were part of a church that belonged to the California Jesus movement.

Sara Zarr

In California, I do like to just chill out and go to the beach, but I love the energy here. I feel very productive when I'm in New York.

Ashley Greene

I've got an extra-specific story about Dr. Dre. I saw him when I was 9 years old in Compton - him and Tupac. They were shooting the second 'California Love' video. My pops had seen him and ran back to the house and got me, put me on his neck, and we stood there watching Dre and Pac in a Bentley.

Kendrick Lamar

When the Oakies left Oklahoma and moved to California, it raised the I.Q. of both states.

Will Rogers

I speak directly to the people, and I know that the people of California want to have better leadership. They want to have great leadership. They want to have somebody that will represent them. And it doesn't matter if you're a Democrat or a Republican, young or old.

Arnold Schwarzenegger

I love California, I practically grew up in Phoenix.

Dan Quayle

There's one Baldessari work I genuinely love and would like to own, maybe because of my Midwestern roots and love of driving alone. 'The backs of all the trucks passed while driving from Los Angeles to Santa Barbara, California, Sunday, 20 January 1963' consists of a grid of 32 small color photographs depicting just what the title says.

Jerry Saltz

Nuclear power plants built in the areas usually thought of as earthquake zones, such as the California coastline, have a surprisingly low risk of damage from those earthquakes. Why? They built anticipating a major quake.

Bill Dedman

The best under-the-radar rivalry is Dodgers-Giants. I had no idea how deep that one was until I moved to California... that one goes waaaaaaaaay back, and both sides absolutely detest each other. Fights in the stands, fights in the parking lot, the whole thing. It's every bit as bitter as Yankees-Red Sox without nearly the same hype.

Bill Simmons

In California, they don't throw their garbage away - they make it into TV shows.

Woody Allen

Earlier today, Arnold Schwarzenegger criticized the California school system, calling it disastrous. Arnold says California's schools are so bad that its graduates are willing to vote for me.

Conan O'Brien

I'm a secret interior decorator. There's a mural on my dining room wall of the railroad tracks at 30th Street Station in Philadelphia. I love having my hometown with me out here in California.

Jill Scott

A Pike, in the California dialect, is a native of Missouri, Arkansas, Northern Texas, or Southern Illinois. The first emigrants that came over the plains were from Pike County, Missouri; but as the phrase, 'a Pike County man,' was altogether too long for this short life of ours, it was soon abbreviated into 'a Pike.'

Bayard Taylor

The biggest problem that we have is that California is being run now by special interests. All of the politicians are not anymore making the moves for the people, but for special interests and we have to stop that.

Arnold Schwarzenegger

I think in the old days, the nexus of weirdness ran through Southern California, and to a degree New York City. I think it's changed so that every bizarre story in the country now has a Florida connection. I don't know why, except it must be some inversion of magnetic poles or something.

Carl Hiaasen

I was in California when this journalist made a blanket
statement about the fact that she did not think that black
men and women had the kind of love relationship that
Rebecca and Nathan had in Sounder.

Cicely Tyson

Arnold Schwarzenegger's publicist told USA Today that
the actor has not ruled out running for governor of
California, saying that he will make a decision soon.
Reportedly Arnold needs that time to learn how to
pronounce 'gubernatorial.'

Jimmy Fallon

Back in the '70s when my friends in California were at
Berkeley, in-state tuition was around $700 a year.

Gail Collins

Because if you don't have a great workforce, a great higher
education system, you're not going to have the next eBay,
the next AmGen, the next, you know, Miasole, and not only
California but America is going to fall behind a whole new

competitive context which is obviously China, India, and other countries.

Meg Whitman

Food should be cheap, and labor should be cheap, and everything should be the same no matter where you go; whether it's a McDonald's in Germany or one in California, it should be the same. And this message is destroying cultures around the world. Needless to say, agriculture goes with it.

Alice Waters

Humility was an important part of the way I grew up. And I found that to be less common when I moved to California. That's not to say humble people don't exist there, but ambition seems really important.

Anna Kendrick

In California in the early Spring, There are pale yellow mornings, when the mist burns slowly into day, The air stings like Autumn, clarifies like pain - Well, I have dreamed this coast myself.

Robert Hass

If it's cross-country ski season, I'll be out doing that, or snowshoeing up in Quebec. In my California home, I go to the local Y and I like doing yoga. It's been hugely beneficial to me in injury avoidance.

Neil Peart

I was in California the first time I heard Michael Jackson wanted to record with me. I was, like, 'Nah, no way, he's too big, it can't be true.' Then I got a call from Michael's people at my hotel telling me he was interested. But I still wasn't believing it - I thought they were setting me up for a TV practical jokes show.

Heavy D

I went West and took part in the strike of the machinists - the Southern Pacific Railroad, the corporation that swung California by its golden tail, that controlled its legislature, its farmers, its preachers, its workers.

Mary Harris Jones

When I came to University of California, San Francisco to work on infectious disease, I looked around to different options, and malaria was particularly interesting and fascinating to me. It's amazing that after 100 years of study of this little parasite, we've not been able to effectively control it.

Joseph DeRisi

My mom was born in San Diego, around Vista. So we've always been California people.

Gracie Gold

My youngest son, who is now the drummer in my band, lives in Brooklyn. My oldest son is about to move out to California, and my daughters are both out of town.

Herbie Mann

My first job in TV was hosting this young teen magazine show, and all these high school teenagers showed up from all over Sacramento, California, and they chose four of us to host the show, two boys and two girls. And of the two girls, I was kind of the perky smart one and the other girl was the pretty one.

Lisa Ling

Family is always first - always, always, always first. As a matter of fact, there was a time when I was thinking of running for Governor in California, and I sat with my family. We all discussed it. It was with the three kids. We sat there, and I polled 40 percent in my own family. I couldn't carry my own family, essentially, and so that was it.

Rob Reiner

Well, I haven't really been able to shoot in California for a while. Little movies yeah, but the big movies we can't shoot there. It's just a shame that Arnold Schwarzenegger can't deliver on this level.

Joel Silver

Most analysts would agree that if all the undocumented immigrants in California were deported in one day, our state would experience a severe economic downturn. This does not even consider the many cultural and spiritual gifts these immigrants bring to our state and nation.

Roger Mahony

I myself was born in Sacramento, California in 1966.

Sarah Zettel

Mr. Tyler acquired Texas by voluntary compact, and Mr. Polk California and New Mexico by successful war.

Robert Toombs

Whenever I get a free day, I drive up to some part of California that looks promising on the map.

Kent McCord

The premise of Nossiter in 'Mondovino' would have been a lot more accurate when I started writing about wine in 1978 than when the movie was made in 2003. When I started, I was enormously critical of California wines, and I thought the entire wine industry was on a real slippery slope.

Robert M. Parker, Jr.

What's important in a cellar is having wines that have a broad range of drinkability, which California Cabernet does. Wines with a broad range of drinkability give you a lot of flexibility; they are the sort of wines that make me feel secure. I think of my wine cellar as security - if the apocalypse comes, I can just go down to the cellar.

Robert M. Parker, Jr.

When I travel round the country, people can't place my accent; if there's someone in the audience, they'll be like, 'You're from Philadelphia', but everyone else will say, 'Where are you from, California?' I get England sometimes - bizarre!

Matthew Quick

Every day there are homeowners in California who will either receive relief so they can stay in their home, or will be in the foreclosure process and potentially lose their home. And that always weighed heavily on my mind.

Kamala Harris

I always wanted to be a Californian. In my wildest dreams, I always liked California - it's the place where oranges grows on trees! Fruit just falls off the trees.

Eric Burdon

Had I stayed longer in some primaries, I would have probably done better in states like Nevada, California, and New Mexico - but I ran out of the money after the second primary in New Hampshire.

Bill Richardson

I'm really into California art from the '60s.

Barry McGee

To say that people would cease to come to California if they would have to pay more taxes is to underestimate the advantages of being in California - mightily.

Warren Beatty

I learned how to sign because when I was growing up in California in order to get into college you needed two semesters of language to get into a University of California school.

Camryn Manheim

I'm from California, but my father, who passed away when I was young, was from Newark. When I was kid, we would go back east and catch Yankees games. His side of the family are big Yankees fans. But, the real connection came in '97 when I moved to New York and became friends with the team.

Carson Daly

Why did we go to war? Why did we pick people from South Carolina, California, and all the places in between to go to a foreign land and risk their lives and have some die? To make sure that Saddam Hussein could do no more damage to the region or us than he has already done.

Lindsey Graham

I spend a lot of time in California, but New York is still my main home. I go to see a lot of theater.

Zeljko Ivanek

I lead an introverted and boring life here in California.

Brian Bosworth

In addition, California spends nearly $1 billion a year in Medi-Cal services for an average of 780,000 illegal immigrants a month, over and above emergency health services.

Elton Gallegly

I mean, I love California, but LA to me is still a strange place.

Scott Speedman

We are selected, but I grew up in California and in San Francisco and there was a system of electing judges.

Stephen Breyer

I had fallen in love with California.

DeForest Kelley

California is full of Mexican culture and Mexican music.

Harry Dean Stanton

The weather in California is so much hotter than it is in England that it's absolutely changed my style. I have many more dresses and shorts than I ever thought I would coming from U.K.! It's so much easier to dress femininely in a warm climate.

Tamsin Egerton

I don't know how many parts I've lost because a lot of the politics in California are very conservative, and I'm fairly outspoken. I always tried to get as much politics in as I could, because I do believe in class struggle, and I think that's what's left out.

James Cromwell

I'm on Governor Gray Davis' California Alliance Towards Education to bring the arts back to high schools.

Sally Kirkland

In California, of all places, entertainment is the key to a vibrant economy. If we do not develop young adults capable of entering that world, the financial base of this state is sure to suffer and impact all of us.

David Cassidy

They have a book of locations, and we would do a story about the Sahara Desert for instance, and in the California book you would find a comparable location, to match that location in California.

Robert Stack

I was never a part of the Actor's Studio, because two friends of mine started it in 1947 and by that time I'd gone to California.

Richard Widmark

I didn't go to L.A. because I wanted to move to California. I went to L.A. to work as an actor.

Bryan Greenberg

Clearly, high energy prices will have a large negative effect on the California economy and could possibly drag the rest of the nation into a recession.

Doug Ose

It's not like I had big dreams to go to California and become an actor. I loved doing my shows at school and community theater, and I probably would have settled in New York because it was closer. I was going to go to NYU.

Christine Taylor

I had sort of exhausted all the avenues playing in Detroit. So again, through the stewardship of my brother, I ended

up in California and went to the Musicians Institute in L.A.
I wanted to get better as a player.

Chad Smith

Coming from New York, you're kind of indoctrinated with
anti-L.A. sentiment, but California is just a really dope
state.

Jesse Williams

UC Merced is the University of California's newest campus
and lies among farm fields in the San Joaquin Valley, 2 1/2
hours east of San Francisco and not far from where I spent
most of my childhood. It's a part of California that has
suffered deeply from the recession with high
unemployment and a skyrocketing home foreclosure rate.

Lester Holt

On another level, I want to mention that I have a strong
Jewish identity and - over the years - have been involved in
several Jewish projects, such as the establishment of a
strong program of Judaic Studies at the University of
California in San Diego.

Walter Kohn

Living here in southern California, I'll miss hearing Rocky Top for an entire week at the end of December. I was actually looking forward to it. Tennessee has a better fight song than Nebraska.

Al Michaels

I was born in Palo Alto, California in 1961.

Eric Allin Cornell

I think my parents were immigrants, you know, so I guess I would be first generation. Growing up in California.

Phillip Lim

I think you're lucky if you discover what you really love at a young age. College wasn't something I was going to do. I wanted to keep acting, and I didn't want to go to New York or California and pound the pavement.

Gary Sinise

The University of Southern California has a wonderful social work department, and I was thrilled to find out that they have a whole veterans' initiative program there. They approached me, and I set up a scholarship that would go to a military-oriented person to learn techniques and skills to better help veterans.

Gary Sinise

Well, it's a little harder in New York. It's not as forgiving to a film crew. You hold up a bunch of New Yorkers who can't cross the street, they're not going to take it well. Southern California? They'll wait. It's cool man. In New York, they're like, 'Are you kidding me? I gotta get to work.'

Matthew Rhys

I'm a California girl, and I'd love to restore a sense of place to Southern California.

Rene Russo

I'm really all about clean eating, lots of fruits and vegetables. It's great, because in California, there are so many farmers' markets, so I always have plenty of fresh produce.

Gracie Gold

And so there I was living in California from Brooklyn, New York, and it was this whole new world for me and I was meeting vegetarians. I thought, let me try this vegetarian thing. I got really into that.

Warren Cuccurullo

One good thing about California is we have quite a broad-based economy. We provide more fruits and vegetables and produce to the United States than any other state. So we have actually the single largest agricultural sector in the country.

Meg Whitman

Certainly the experiences of Seth and his relationship to his parents and his point of view of the world are very similar to my own and very much based on my experiences at the University of Southern California.

Josh Schwartz

Nothing is wrong with California that a rise in the ocean level wouldn't cure.

Ross MacDonald

I was 17 when I left the small Maine town where I'd grown up. I wanted to do something I thought was important with my life, so I headed to California and didn't look back.

Patrick Dempsey

My dad couldn't connect to my wanting to be a filmmaker. He was very connected in entertainment, and through him I met Steven Spielberg and got rides on his private plane to California. I'd see Spielberg's people reading scripts. I was like, 'That's what I want to be when I grow up.'

Doug Liman

Growing up in California, I obviously knew about our deep connections with the Japanese.

John Roos

Some of the most exciting space education in the country is not coming out of Washington or New York or California or even Texas. It's coming from a place in Kansas called the Cosmosphere.

Eugene Cernan

I was in New York. Hitchcock was in California. He rang me to make a report on his progress and said, I'm having trouble. I've just sacked my second screenwriter.

Patricia Highsmith

Westerns was why I got into the business. I grew up on a small farm in California and all I ever wanted to do was to play gangsters and cowboys in movies.

Brion James

A lot of people don't understand how cargo coming into our ports matters, not just to Southern California but to every single congressional district. I want to educate on that issue.

Janice Hahn

What I wonder is what would happen in California, say, if all the Mexicans left from one day to the next?

Alma Guillermoprieto

I'm really into California art from the '60s. I like a lot of

Bay Area artists, like Nathan Oliveira and Bruce Conner.

Barry McGee

In the rural South, 'Bubba' is like how people say 'dude' in California. It's a name for a regular Southern man. I know a Chinese Bubba, a black Bubba.

Bubba Sparxxx

And as part of my activity there, he had indicated he wanted me to work with him on that and conduct the various technical tests. And so a few months later I moved from Southern California up to the Monterey Peninsula where I still live today.

John Sexton

My wife and I have spent half our lives, half our adult lives, trying to save special parts of California.

Pete McCloskey

I sort of lived half my life in California, half in England, so I am, I suppose, a little bit American.

Alice Eve

I left Chicago many years ago to move to California. You can't help but live a healthy lifestyle here if you want to fit in. I find myself eating chicken and salad and chicken and salad and salad and chicken, like a monk.

James Belushi

I was not a Southern California girl. I hated having my photograph taken. I felt shy and embarrassed around famous people.

Allegra Huston

Our original idea was to help three or four hundred candidates in the first election run for the Ohio State legislature and the California legislature around the country.

Pete du Pont

I'm originally from southern California, so I, like, say 'like', like, a lot. I've been trying to scrub any traces of Valley Girl from my speech since I moved to New York, but it's, like, totally way harder than anyone thinks, you know?

Mara Wilson

As I said in my state of the state address, we can no longer rely on gaming and sales taxes to pay our way. Indian gaming next door in California is eroding our major industry in Nevada.

Kenny Guinn

There are certain things that are inherently scarce. For example, there is only a certain amount of beachfront property in California. It is going to be scarce, it is going to be expensive.

Ralph Merkle

I grew up in Southern California, Simi Valley. I've lived in the same house all my life.

Jason Dolley

Growing up in England, you're sort of spoiled, in a way. You sort of take it for granted that within a half-hour's drive, you could be walking around a stately home from the 1700s. It's not very hard to do - in California, you've got to take a flight!

Rupert Friend

It was not possible to film in California, because all the areas are heavily built up now. Coming to Cape Town is an invitation to step into the past and recreate Los Angeles of the 1930s.

Robert Towne

California lacks a lot of the rules and restrictions the East has. Every house is a different style, different material, different color. There's a lot of craziness out there.

Parker Stevenson

I'm doing my part, building plants at a record rate, having historic conservation levels. The only people not doing their part is the federal government that is siding with the energy companies against the interests of the people of California.

Gray Davis

So it was flawed in that it didn't require California to have a first claim on the power plants. It deregulated part of the market, but not all of the market.

Gray Davis

There's no question that California, in the last three or four years, has been privileged to add disproportionately to the economic growth of America, and to contribute to its technological productivity.

Gray Davis

I love California. I love Hollywood.

Dwight Henry

I was producing demos for a band that was called Physical Ed. Out of production of demos I went and did a few jam sessions with then in Northern California clubs, but I never actually toured with them.

Ronnie Montrose

I continue to be a photographer; I have enjoyed fishing and hunting with a close friend; and have owned two ranches, first in northern California and then in the state of Washington.

Douglass North

There was a three hour differential in performances because the sponsor insisted it be done live for California. You would go on at 8 pm in New York but you would also have to go on at 8 p.m. in California. That meant coming back in to do the show at 11 p.m.

Dick York

Then years back, when I moved to California, I happened to see a book about fashions of 19th-century Victorian England, only four pages of which was devoted to the dress of the working class.

Martin Cruz Smith

California club pop chirper Dev's debut is as stark as it is sweet. This is owed partly to the casually giddy lightness of her talk-singing - familiar from her slizzered 2010 cameo on Far East Movement's smash 'Like a G6,' and around-the way-girl frisky like 1980s Latin freestyle.

Chuck Eddy

Southern California, they have been amazing. They're totally with us.

Chita Rivera

Wherever I am, I will embrace the life and the lifestyle. I've lived in Hollywood before, and we've moved into the old neighbourhood in West Hollywood. I love California.

John Barrowman

One way to bring down crime in the state of California and every state in the union is to have an enforceable border. That means let's build that border fence. When people want to come into this country, let's ask them to knock on the front door.

Duncan Hunter

A guy friend and I went to California Pizza Kitchen, and a group of pretty girls came over to us and said, 'You guys are gay, right?'

Chad Michael Murray

When I came to New York in 1949, there was already an entire fresh avant-garde film movement blooming in New York and California. It was a very, very exciting period!

Jonas Mekas

When I first saw California, it was extraordinary. Because I came from old, black, dark England, still recovering from World War II. I grew up with bomb sites everywhere.

Geoffrey West

There were a lot of kids from Puerto Rico at my high school in Florida; people always assumed I was Puerto Rican. Even now in California, I get talked to on the street in Spanish constantly!

Torrey DeVitto

There is a big cry in California to stop everyone from running to Canada.

Wayne Rogers

I never pictured myself in California. I just thought I would be a character actress in New York on the stage. I never really had that stardom goal; I just wanted to be able to work as an actress and not as a waitress.

Rhea Perlman

I guess I really always wanted to act. When I was seven, I actually had the opportunity to come out to California. I've always really loved playing a part, playing a character and being someone else.

Madison Davenport

We never really wanted to play in California.

Santiago Durango

I wanted to be a theater actress, but I thought it would be easier to get to New York and the theater if I had a name than if I just walked the streets as a little girl from California.

Gloria Stuart

I went back to the States and started at a small newspaper in Riverside County, California, covering the police; I was making $280 a week covering the police.

John Pomfret

Donald Beardslee is set for execution this week in California. His crimes were about twenty years ago, but it will be the first execution in California in quite some time.

Catherine Crier

I consider myself to be more real-sized than most of the actresses in California and in show business. They're very small. They're like miniature people.

Jane Krakowski

I have family dotted everywhere - Dad's in California; I've got aunts in Scotland and Virginia; family in Kansas City; family in Manchester and London.

Hayley Atwell

When I came back to California in the early '60s I was hanging out with Jimmy Bowen, Phil Spector, and I wanted to be a record producer and work with other artists.

Johnny Rivers

I have three adopted children with Phil, and for years I was fighting in court with him over being able to see my kids. I was always going back and forth to California, going to court, and I was never able to get a project going.

Ronnie Spector

I think it's a tremendous opportunity, particularly given the complexion of the overall voter structure in California. It's very hard for a Republican to get elected.

Mike Curb

As I was leaving graduate school in 1974, I was recruited to join a fledgling SETI project at the Hat Creek Observatory in California, mainly because I knew how to program an ancient PDP8/S computer that had been donated to the project.

Jill Tarter

I'm from Southern California, so I feel much more comfortable with a golf club in my hand than I do a weapon.

Bert Blyleven

I'm no romantic, surfing, California boy. I like reading, writing, philosophizing. Scheming. I've been doing some exploration of the inner space.

Henry Hopper

When I was filming 'Buffy the Vampire Slayer' in America, for a couple of weeks beforehand we would always fit in a family holiday in California.

Anthony Head

I didn't finish high school - left home when I was 15. I moved away to Fresno and worked as a grocery clerk. I went to college part-time at California State Fresno, and then ended up finishing in two and a half years because I wanted to get on with things.

Joy Covey

I grew up in northern California in a town called Fairfield, which is kind of exactly between San Francisco and Sacramento, a small suburb. And I'm the youngest of five children.

Tracy K. Smith

I'm also performing regularly in Southern California with two bands. As a solo artist doing acoustic sets and a member of the Jenerators, my rock n roll band that has been around for a long time now.

Bill Mumy

The debt ceiling at some point has to be raised. I don't think there's anybody that questions the fact that if we ended up getting in a situation where the U.S. government was sending out IOUs like the state of California did at one point, that ends up creating quite a brand problem for our country.

Bob Corker

I moved to California not to pursue acting but to get out of Albuquerque.

Minka Kelly

Each time that I have two or three days off, I'm off somewhere in California.

Lizzie Brochere

Brian really kicked back on his own when Amanda was a baby. We had a long talk about it, and he was spending a lot of time in California working there and he didn't really want to spend all his time out there and have his children and his wife on the East Coast.

Erika Slezak

And looking at the landslides, you saw how Gore beat Bush so substantially in California.

Mike Curb

We have enough to worry about with what's happening in our nation to worry about what's happening in California. Keep your feet grounded in your own backyard and together we're going to build communities that work.

Sher Valenzuela

University of California students can look forward to the same authoritarian management style Secretary Napolitano brought to the Department of Homeland Security, hardly a bastion of free speech and open government.

Doug LaMalfa

California is going to be quite good for the Democrats. But the rest of the country is a draw.

Stuart Rothenberg

I just didn't know what the heck I wanted to do with my life, so I drove out to California and got really lucky.

Krista Allen

In my district, California 14, we have about 4,000 families who are on food stamps, but some of my colleagues have thousands and thousands more. Yet, they somehow feel like crusaders, like heroes, when they vote to cut food stamps.

Jackie Speier

I moved to L.A. after my landlord in Brooklyn tripled my rent. I spent months looking for other places to move to in New York, then one day I was in California eating a grapefruit, and I was like, 'This is what they taste like?' So I decided to move to L.A. and build a studio in my house.

Dave Sitek

People here always said to me, 'Why would you leave civilization to go to a place like Fiji?' Fiji is a far more civilized place than California or New York City.

Raymond Burr

My mother was very involved with Cesar Chavez's work on behalf of the migrant farm workers in California.

Caitlin Flanagan

I became a Republican in the summer of 1972. I was involved in running President Nixon's re-election campaign in California and became part of his administration at the start of his second term.

Ed Rollins

I was born in Orange County - in Santa Ana. My dad is from California. I was raised on the East Coast. My first two years were in California, but I claim East Coast. I'm sorry, I don't rep California.

Michael B. Jordan

Life in California is beautiful.

Oscar Nunez

I'm a typical California boy.

Gary Lockwood

Tia and I have been together for 10 years. Our relationship is not just something that happened overnight. She was with me when I moved to California. I had nothing, and she was established, who had all this money, but she didn't care. That's how I knew she was real.

Cory Hardrict

In California, for so long now, our families have been struggling in this economic environment, and Dianne Feinstein, been in office nearly half a century, is out of touch of what women and families are going through in California.

Elizabeth Emken

When you look at a Congress that has an 84 percent disapproval rating, that means that for the most part, the people of this country, and certainly California, are looking for new leadership.

Elizabeth Emken

As I got into my teens, I started reading better books, beginning with the Beats and then the hippie writers, people like Wallace Stegner up in Northern California, and all the political New Journalism stuff, the Boys on the Bus dudes and Ken Kesey.

Stephen Gaghan

I was 19 when I got my first passport as an adult. I had moved from California to New York City and was living out of a suitcase, staying with friends. I'd just finished filming my first movie, 'Ordinary People,' but I didn't know whether acting was what I wanted to do with my life.

Timothy Hutton

I'm a third generation Californian, and there's a lot of talented, good-looking guys in California, so I'm just happy to be working and lucky to be working.

Scott Eastwood

What is Southern California but an ever-changing dreamscape backdrop for the postmodern ideal? The psychology of the postmodern world is the continual state of change as we live in its idealist manufactured dream, built by developers.

John Van Hamersveld

I lived in Arizona, and I thought Florida was in California because I thought oranges came from the same place.

Jennifer Rubin

I had my airplane, and I'd use it as a car whenever I could. If the drive was going to be longer than an hour, I was flying the plane instead. And in California, it's really easy to have a drive longer than an hour.

Jake Busey

It was always my dream, getting to America? Honestly, I couldn't figure America as being real. Because it was on discs or in the movies. I was shocked when I first went to Detroit. I thought everybody was rich. Everybody had green lawns, no fences, because everyone has a hedge, you know. Of course, the movies are always shot in California.

Ian McLagan

Likewise, with solar, especially here in California, we're discovering that the 80 solar farm schemes that are going forward want to basically bulldoze 1,000 sq. mi. of southern California desert. Well, as an environmentalist, we would rather that didn't happen.

Stewart Brand

Judy Garland's father was gay. That seems to be the consensus. They left Minnesota and went to California because he got caught with some boy backstage.

Judy Davis

Ronald Reagan, of course, was a Republican governor of California who went through a painful defeat in the 1976 presidential race before winning four years later.

Michael Medved

I grew up in Northern California, so the hippies were still around. My father and mother were very Republican, very strait-laced and very uptight, but my uncles were hippies.

Grant Show

The Committee supports the idea that there should be, within the University of California, a campus which puts particular emphasis on the education of undergraduates within the framework of a College system.

Abraham Robinson

We would go down to Riverside, California, which is very poor now, but that's where my grandfather grew up. He grew up during the Depression in Riverside.

Greta Gerwig

For 'Breaking Bad,' our offices were in the ugliest building in Burbank, California. Which, if you know Burbank, is really saying something.

Peter Gould

I don't think the state of California realized there would be this many people here caught up in the freeway system.

Richard Grieco

The first time I came to California was in January 2013, when I auditioned for 'Vampire Academy.'

Lucy Fry

I started with California, and I did not like it. I flew over to Seattle, and I did not like it much. I felt like Iowa is the place - I like the people and the environment.

Liang Chow

Probably the first time I was a boss was when I was associate dean of the graduate school at the University of Southern California. I was in my early 30s.

Ruth J. Simmons

I almost threw up the first time I set foot inside the University of California, San Francisco's Comprehensive Care Center and joined the stream of thin, slow-moving, low-voiced, gray-skinned people. I didn't want to be one of the pitied, the struck-down.

Kelly Corrigan

I moved from Philadelphia to California when I was 25, after traveling abroad for a year. I thought I'd come home eventually and settle down, but I didn't.

Kelly Corrigan

My dad signed me up for some acting classes at a place in Honolulu, and there I got to audition for some L.A.-based talent agents. I got a few 'callbacks' and so my mom and I decided to fly to California and check it out!

Maxim Knight

When I was 11 years old, I was bullied. It mainly started when I moved to California to pursue my dreams of being an actress. Kids back home in Texas, who I thought were my friends, were saying things behind my back. They said that I would never make it because I wasn't talented or pretty enough to be on TV.

Raini Rodriguez

A long time ago, when I was married, in the beginning it was bliss. I eloped after one month, and I married for security. I thought, 'I finally met a man who loves God and comes from a great family. I'm working, I love God, and I'm out here in California by myself, and I've met this great man.' So, I said yes. And we eloped.

Tichina Arnold

I'm running for controller to ensure our government reflects the values of the people of California and increases prosperity by managing our finances smartly, efficiently and effectively.

John Perez

If a voter initiative can deny gay people access to traditional representative, democratic processes, then in California, any other small, historically disadvantaged minority group can also be denied the right of representative.

John Perez

I think from the time I was a kid I've been an entertainer. I've always had the ability to play characters. When I came to California, I was overwhelmed that you could do this and get paid for it, make a living on it, and be creative within this art form.

Matt Schulze

I came out to California to live with my mom in Orange County for a while, and then I came up to Hollywood. I had just turned nineteen. I took an acting class at Playhouse West and decided, 'Wow, I think I can do this!' I studied really hard for three years before I got an agent.

Jamie Anne Allman

I had a weird high school because I graduated early when I was 16. I moved out to California, but I was only there for freshman and sophomore year, and I was a bit of a brainiac.

Shanley Caswell

I'm wary of the whole Los Angeles scene. I'm a California kid, but there's a difference between California and Los Angeles. L.A. is urban. California is restorative.

Jason Lewis

Lots of TV shows say that they are like doing a movie every week, but 'JAG' truly was a huge show. Lots of once-in-a-lifetime opportunities, like being launched off an aircraft carrier and being welcomed by military bases all over California.

Patrick Labyorteaux

I was in a music class when I was little, and they discovered I had a talent and could sing. From there, I joined this singing troupe in California, and I would just go sing at festivals in this girl group and perform as much as I could.

Vanessa Morgan

I made a decision to live outside the city in northern California. My agent said to me, 'Kid, you're going to make a mint in television movies.' He positioned me, and we picked really good projects, and I cornered that market. They were 20-day projects.

Mare Winningham

A lot of the people in Northern California and parts of Oregon have decided that we are not on the same page as San Francisco and Portland and Los Angeles. I don't know if six states is a solution because is Washington, D.C. and the rest of the country really going to give California 10 new senators?

Doug LaMalfa

In the fall of the year 2000, there just happened to be a decision point when they asked me to become Chief Executive Officer of the company. It was a time when, as you remember, we were starting to have some real problems in the California energy markets.

Jeffrey Skilling

And now, of course this is another thing I didn't count on, that now as the governor of the state of California, I am selling California worldwide. You see that? Selling.

Arnold Schwarzenegger

Women are the engine driving the growth in California's economy. Women make California's economy unique.

Arnold Schwarzenegger

Southern California is a nice place, if you could cut out the show-business cancer. It just keeps spreading.

P. J. O'Rourke

Well, I think that California has had a history of always spending more money than it takes in.

Arnold Schwarzenegger

I'd like to talk to Arnold Schwarzenegger, 'cause I live in California and I just want to see that canned, chemical filled body in my office.

Henry Rollins

Notre Dame is the one school that has a national recruiting base, from Florida to Texas to California.

Lou Holtz

The California crunch really is the result of not enough power-generating plants and then not enough power to power the power of generating plants.

George W. Bush

My biggest extravagances are also investments. I have several houses in California, a house in Nashville, an office complex, and I bought the old home place in Tennessee. They are different places for me to write, but I can turn right around and sell them.

Dolly Parton

California is an unbelievable state. One day I might be in a spiritual place like Joshua Tree, then before I know it, I'm eating groovy sushi in a mini-mall. I'm a Cali girl through and through.

Drew Barrymore

For 25 years, it has been my privilege to represent the city of San Francisco and the great state of California; to work to strengthen our vibrant middle class; to secure opportunity and equality.

Nancy Pelosi

It feels wistful to imagine a time when people didn't go about their daily routine with the assumption that at any moment another massive media technology will be dumped on us by some geek in California.

Douglas Coupland

Growing up in northern California has had a big influence on my love and respect for the outdoors. When I lived in Oakland, we would think nothing of driving to Half Moon Bay and Santa Cruz one day and then driving to the foothills of the Sierras the next day.

Tom Hanks

When future archaeologists dig up the remains of California, they're going to find all of those gyms their scary-looking gym equipment, and they're going to assume that we were a culture obsessed with torture.

Douglas Coupland

California is a queer place in a way, it has turned its back on the world, and looks into the void Pacific. It is absolutely selfish, very empty, but not false, and at least, not full of false effort.

D. H. Lawrence

The Reagans were dear friends for many years, even when he was governor of California. Nancy appreciated a lot of Philippine-made things.

Imelda Marcos

Since I had my gastric bypass surgery in 1998, I eat like a bird. Unfortunately, that bird is a California condor.

Roseanne Barr

Adultery - which is the only grounds for divorce in New York - is not grounds for divorce in California. As a matter of fact, adultery in Southern California is grounds for marriage.

Allan Sherman

If you want to surf, move to Hawaii. If you like to shop, move to New York. If you like acting and Hollywood, move to California. But if you like college football, move to Texas.

Ricky Williams

No matter where you put me, I don't care if it is North Carolina, Florida, California, New York City; I'm going to be who I am.

Chris Paul

The truth is in California you can't build a new manufacturing facility, and businesses are leaving in droves because of bad government policy.

Carly Fiorina

I'm meant for California.

Lauren Conrad

My family belongs to a tennis club in Valencia, California, so I always go there. I play a lot of tennis with my dad and swim. And I like to go to the gym there.

Ashley Tisdale

It doesn't rain at all in California. Once a month, a man drives through spraying Evian.

Hugh Laurie

The American model was celebrated by Thatcherites and New Labour alike, California worshipped as the model of the future, 'Anglo-Saxon' embalmed as the fitting metaphor for the shared Anglo-American legacy, Europe denigrated and the rest of the world ignored.

Martin Jacques

I like owning dirt. You know, I spent a lot of time broke when I moved to California. So deep in my soul is still this idea of being unemployed. To me, owning land means you could sell it at some point and have money.

George Clooney

I'd like to be able to use Storm's powers for good, like have it rain more in Southern California. We could do with it.

Halle Berry

I've grown to love California: It's the dream of every
English musician to come here and work in the sunshine.
To walk up Sunset Boulevard, knowing you're going to
make music - that's it.

Noel Gallagher

Well I teach in the History of Consciousness Department at
the University of California, Santa Cruz. So that's my
primary work. I lecture on various campuses and in various
communities across the country and other parts of the
world.

Angela Davis

I think it's best if there's an amendment that goes on the
ballot where the people can weigh in. Every time this issue
has gone on the ballot, the people have voted to retain the
traditional definition of marriage as recently as California
in 2008.

Michele Bachmann

My grandmother raised five children during the Depression

by herself. At 50, she threw her sewing machine into the back of a pickup truck and drove from North Dakota to California. She was a real survivor, so that's my stock. That's how I want my kids to be too.

Michelle Pfeiffer

I don't want to look like Connecticut, no offense, I don't want to look like Oklahoma, I don't want to look like California. I want to be uniquely Texas. And that's not to diss anybody else.

Rick Perry

I was born in Africa. I came to California because it's really where new technologies can be brought to fruition, and I don't see a viable competitor.

Elon Musk

I moved to California when I was twelve and I got a video camera and made little movies because I didn't have any friends yet. I would force my sister to make these movies with me - which became my YouTube channel.

Dylan O'Brien

I am the ultimate California girl, which is funny, being that I'm Canadian.

Pamela Anderson

Southern California, where the American Dream came too true.

Lawrence Ferlinghetti

A lot of the stories I was brought up on had to do with extreme actions - leaving everything behind, crossing the trackless wastes, and in those stories the people who stayed behind and had their settled ways - those people were not the people who got the prize. The prize was California.

Joan Didion

A West Virginia 10 is a California 4. Or at least that's what legend tells us: The Legend of Dr. Feelgood. Plastic surgery has a permanent home here, which is why Nancy Pelosi loves our Botoxed beaches. Beverly Hills looks like a moving Madame Tussauds.

Ben Shapiro

I read the Life magazine articles about free love and free dope in California. At age 20 I drove to Los Angeles.

Glenn Frey

I love being a gypsy. Home is between New York and California.

Erin Wasson

I had just arrived in New York from California. I was nineteen years old and excited beyond belief. I was an art student and an acting student and behaved as most young actors did - meaning that there was no such thing as a good actor, 'cause you yourself hadn't shown up yet.

Robert Redford

I have worked with this red all over the world - in Japan, California, France, Britain, Australia - a vein running round the earth. It has taught me about the flow, energy and life that connects one place with another.

Andy Goldsworthy

Who today is willing to say that Texas and California and

the remainder of the Southwest would be better off if they were governed by Mexico?

Stephen Ambrose

Patagonia, a large apparel manufacturer based in Ventura, California, has organized itself as a 'B-corporation.' That's a for-profit company whose articles of incorporation require it to take into account the interests of workers, the community, and the environment, as well as shareholders.

Robert Reich

My father has positional vertigo, and if he flies he gets really dizzy, so he has to drive out to California, which he does a couple times a year. We talk, but we e-mail mostly.

Ben Affleck

I run three to four times a week. I go down to Orange County in California and I run all the time... all the time. You see the oceans, the trees. I like running in hot weather. I like to sweat and get all those toxins out of my system. I thoroughly enjoy it.

Sugar Ray Leonard

We opened the first Men's Wearhouse in Houston in August 1973, then a store a year for 10 years in Texas. In the early 1980s I opened a store in the San Francisco Bay Area. Within the year, the Texas economy was in total disarray. We were facing Chapter 11, and if not for the California store, we might not have survived.

George Zimmer

I like California but I'm dyed-in-the-wool Oklahoma. I see a deer in L.A., and everybody's standing around it taking pictures. Back home, that's the enemy!

Blake Shelton

I was born in California. When I was six, we moved to a small town in northern Indiana called Mishawaka.

Adam Driver

I looked along the San Juan Islands and the coast of California, but I couldn't find the palette of green, granite, and dark blue that you can only find in Maine.

Parker Stevenson

When I came home for the summer after my first year of college, I told my mother that my best friend and I were driving to California. She laughed out loud - 2,000 miles in a what? Well, my best friend had an old Chevy. What could go wrong?

Jane Smiley

I really appreciate the many neighbourhoods of Berkeley. There is still the butcher, the baker and the candlestick maker. And it has the University of California, which is the greatest gift, to my mind, to be close to it. It keeps the place alive.

Alice Waters

I speak as much Spanish as anyone who has grown up in Southern California or Texas or Arizona. I had my three years of high-school Spanish and a couple of semesters in college.

Will Ferrell

Having lived in the arid deserts of Southern California since the 1970s, my interest in water conservation is a very personal concern. Water! The source of life! Some people are squandering the world's most precious resource while others have too little clean water to drink.

Eric Burdon

First and foremost I am a chef, whether behind the stove at one of my Northern California restaurants or for the past 15 years in front of the camera on my Food Network cooking shows. Creating new dishes and flavor combinations that bring cooks and our restaurant guests pleasure is my job and I love it.

Tyler Florence

I grew up with the Blind Boys' music. My family owns a music store in Claremont, California, called The Claremont Folk Music Center. I grew up with a heavy diet of gospel, folk, and blues because those are kind of the cornerstones of traditional American music.

Ben Harper

Really, truly, try to figure out what your palate is all about. If you've determined that you don't like dirty old stinky wine - old-world flavors - you probably like new-world fruit bombs. Stick to Shirazes and California Cabernets or Zinfandels.

Gary Vaynerchuk

I love living in California and being able to go to the beach or go to the woods.

Tracy Chapman

Right out of the University of California I had passed the bar, but Colorado was one of those places where anybody could come and nobody would ask what your background was or how long you had been here. So I took to the place with a liking.

Richard Lamm

I went to UCF in Florida in Orlando. I went for advertising and public relations. I moved out to California my senior year because I knew I wanted to be an actor, but I also wanted to finish school and get my degree. I took mainly a bunch of criminal justice courses online for the last year because that's all that they offered.

Drew Seeley

When I first arrived in America, the very first place I came was California, and I rented a house in Trance, which is about half an hour from Malibu.

Olivia Newton-John

I was very aware of performers who have a persona, whether it's Siouxsie Sioux or Patti Smith or Lydia Lunch, and I'm just this middle-class girl coming from a more conventional upbringing, this California person. But in a way I felt like it's important to represent the normal.

Kim Gordon

But if you go over the line, you don't want to get stuck in a Nevada State court room. Honestly, because Nevada has been doing a good job of putting California criminals in jail. I mean, we couldn't put OJ in jail, but they did. We couldn't put Paris Hilton in jail, but they did.

James Belushi

One of the great things about Lanai is that the weather is always fabulous. Always 82 degrees and sunny. The problem is that, like California now, Lanai needs more water.

Larry Ellison

I think California has some very good looking women... I know Stephanie Seymour is from San Diego, and I know Josie Maran - who's my very good friend - she's from

Northern California. So I think California produces some good looking women, for sure.

Marisa Miller

Album sales have collapsed, with few artists making money from albums; touring is more lucrative. But I'm 53 now and won't be able to tour forever, so a logical step is to get into writing film scores. Trouble is, you need to be somewhere which has a big film industry - another reason why I'm thinking about living in California.

Gary Numan

The value of an arts education is widely accepted, especially in California.

Gavin Newsom

Unless action is taken soon - unless we can display the same vision of that earlier period - we will lose the treasure of California's open space and environmental beauty.

Adam Schiff

The travel and tourism industry is the lifeblood of many

states around the country - including Florida, California, New York and Nevada, to name a few.

Mark Foley

As a kid growing up in Southern California, I was a frequent visitor to the Disneyland and developed a deep love of the magic and wonder of Disney.

Kidada Jones

Hot, dry katabatic winds, like the south foehn in Europe, the sharav in the Middle East, and the Santa Ana of Southern California, are all believed to have a decided effect on human behavior and are associated with such health problems as migraines, depression, lethargy, and moodiness. Some scientists say that this is a myth.

Tim Cahill

Los Angeles was an impression of failure, of disappointment, of despair, and of oddly makeshift lives. This is California? I thought.

Joseph Barbera

We can put our head in the sand and continue to lose jobs overseas and to other states, or we can say, 'You know what? We are not going to lose another job from California, and we're going to be the very best place to start and grow a business.' So I'll be the chief sales officer for California businesses.

Meg Whitman

The reason I moved to California the first time was to build the Cobra. I thought it was stupid to have a 1918 taxicab engine in what Europeans like to call a performance car when a little American V-8 could do the job better.

Carroll Shelby

A small-time hoodlum who had spent most of the 1960s at San Quentin State Prison in California, the 30-year-old Bryant claimed that he hijacked Flight 97 under orders from his higher-ups in the Black Panther Party; he said his mission was to arrange for the purchase of bazookas to aid the organization's struggle against oppression.

Brendan I. Koerner

Since 2006, we have surpassed Alaska, Oklahoma, Louisiana, and California in oil production to become the second largest oil-producing state in the nation, trailing only Texas. In 2012, North Dakota produced more than 245 million barrels of oil and provided nearly 11 percent of all U.S. output.

John Hoeven

I did this class when I first moved to California. It was a 'Kids on Camera' class up in the Bay Area. That was good for just getting me excited in acting and everything. Then once I started working down L.A., I just stuck to my acting coach, and she helps me prepare with auditions and that sort of thing.

Bridgit Mendler

I went to California at a perfect time... when many of those people that I had admired so much in films were not working that much. They had free time on their hands to talk to... me, and they liked me because I knew so much about them.

Robert Osborne

I don't live in New York or California. I'm in the grocery store, at the park with my kids, and I'm a normal person. I'm feeding my chickens and agonizing about my next book!

Sarah Dessen

It is unacceptable that immigrants, including children, are shackled and detained in deplorable conditions. And it is unacceptable that already this year immigrants have died by the dozens in the California desert or in other parts of the Southwest.

Roger Mahony

Arnold has succeeded at every level, and I believe he is the only person that can unite the people of this state and lead California from its current dysfunctional condition to the bright future that all residents long for.

Mary Bono

I was a lot more cultured than the other kids in my high school. Because I traveled, I understood different cultures and had a more worldly view. Most of the people I went to high school with had never been outside of California.

Tony Hawk

Well, I think it's real important that people understand, first and foremost, those of us that have lived in Arizona or in southern California, we have a very diverse population. The Hispanic population has been part of all of our lives since we've been born here or since we've grown up here.

Jan Brewer

One of my reasons for living in California is its close proximity to Mexico. The Latin influence is in every corner of the community. My love of Spanish music hasn't wavered since the '50s. I could hear the blues voicing from the Flamanco families and I always dig for inspiration in Latin music.

Eric Burdon

I'm in California, and that usually leans Democratic, and that's usually where I lean anyway... I would lean Democrat; I would lean Obama.

Axl Rose

I didn't want to give up my Illinois driver's license and was unaware that was a crime. It is, by the way, in the state of California. Lesson learned. I technically broke a law, so technically I deserve whatever I get.

Patrick Stump

Well, my thoughts about California are kind of mythological. To me, as well as being a real place, it's a place where people go to find something - to find happiness or to realize their dreams. So it has that kind of quality of heroism and heartache, and Australia has that, as well.

Colin Hay

I got into medical school at the University of California in San Francisco and did well. A lot of smart kids in medical school, and believe me, I wasn't not nearly the smartest one, but I was the most focused and the happiest kid in medical school. In 1979, I graduated as the valedictorian and was honored with the Gold Cane Award.

Richard Carmona

'Eyes Wide Open' took shape from two real life events straight from my own past. One was the sad suicide of my young nephew, a troubled kid, who was found at the bottom of a landmark cliff in central California. The second was a chance encounter forty years ago with none other than, ahem, Charles Manson!

Andrew Gross

Back 20 years ago, I was recording with Bruce Springsteen, and his producer called me and said I had to be in the studio the next day to finish the sessions, and I couldn't. I had to be in court, in California. All this took like 10 years out of my life.

Ronnie Spector

However, don't let these statistics mislead you, gang violence is not limited to California and or big urban areas - that might have been true a while ago but it is no longer the case today.

Bob Filner

The big political news, Arnold Schwarzenegger announced he's running for governor of California, and already, people are chanting, 'Four more vowels, four more vowels.'

Craig Kilborn

In the photographs themselves there's a definite contrast between the figures and the location - I like that kind of California backyard look; clapboard houses, staircases outdoors.

Helmut Newton

Before I joined professional baseball, I started umpiring in San Diego, California. I worked 155 games in a five-month season. For three years in a row, I was working tripleheaders on Saturday and doubleheaders on Sunday.

Doug Harvey

Oh, yeah. I grew up in Southern California in the 1960's. It was very different. I was an only child as opposed to having siblings. My brothers all lived with my step-mom. I am very close to them, but we were not raised in the same house.

David Cassidy

I'm Mexican-American. My dad was actually born in Mexico. He was raised up there, and he came back and forth to America pretty much his whole teenage years. My mom is from Sacramento, California, and she's a blonde-haired, blue-eyed girl. She's a whitey.

Ryan Guzman

For me, California is all about rest, relaxation, space.

Karen O

My Christmas present to myself each year is to see how much air travel can open up the world and take me to places as far from sheltered California and Japan as possible.

Pico Iyer

My grandmother was a teacher, my sister was a teacher, my daughter was a teacher and is now a superintendent in northern California, and my son-in-law is a high school principal. I am surrounded.

Loni Anderson

I was raised in California, so this whole New York winter thing is completely new for me. I've already justified buying seven coats!

Blake Lively

I have the largest collection of Hulk memorabilia in the world - everything from toilet paper, wallpaper, bicycles - all boxed up at my house in Northern California. I've had it for so long, I think it might be time to sell it.

Lou Ferrigno

I love driving; driving along the California coastline is the best drive in the world.

Al Jardine

You can look at the state of California, which is on a pathway to destruction because they expanded government too much, thinking that there would always be someone to pay for it.

Greg Abbott

I used to work at this store called Music Plus in San Clemente, California, when I was growing up, and then they became Blockbuster Music, and, like, you had to get a haircut to work there, and at the time I had some pretty long hair. So after that policy was imposed, I knew that was going to be my last summer working there.

Jorge Garcia

Now on a personal level with things like the California Tax Commission... I really think if people started banding together and saying no to this it could snowball and that could really help.

Joe Eszterhas

Instead, California is one of only 10 states that provides in-state college and university tuition to illegal immigrants. That's grossly unfair to a legal high school student who moves out of California for a year, then returns to attend college.

Elton Gallegly

I guess I never really had a high school experience. I went for about a month, and on the first day one of my friends got punched in the eye. It was Southern California Public High School. Needless to say, I wasn't there for long.

Penn Badgley

There is a lot of lip service paid in this Congress and downtown at the White House about family values and small business. Who better represents family values and small business than the fishermen and women on the Oregon and California coast.

Peter DeFazio

The Middle East is literally going up in flames, as is

California, and Katrina's problems haven't been solved, and Congress' response is to criticize Federal judges.

Alcee Hastings

One of the things I had a hard time getting used to when I came to California in '78 was Santa Claus in shorts.

Dennis Franz

People actually enjoy it when it rains in San Diego because we never get it. It's a nice change of pace. When you live in Southern California, everybody says, 'It's so expensive there.' I tell them, 'It's just a very expensive weather tax.'

Steve Finley

Then I left that school and I went to Cerritos College, which was in southern California; they had one of the best big band programs in the country at the time.

Bobby McFerrin

In 1969, I wrote a musical called 'Mother Earth.' It was a rock musical with an ecology theme. We did it at the South Coast Repertory Theatre in Southern California where I was a member. It was a smash hit in this small theater.

Toni Tennille

Like my colleague, I represent a large Assyrian community in central California, one of the largest concentrations of Assyrian Americans anywhere in the United States.

Dennis Cardoza

I am a big Vespa enthusiast, and I enjoy the state park aspect of California. It's awfully nice to ride my little scooter through the mountains and then wind up at the ocean.

Deirdre Lovejoy

I pledged California to a Northern Republic and to a flag that should have no treacherous threads of cotton in its warp, and the audience came down in thunder.

Thomas Starr King

I'm a full-blooded Mexican. My mother was born in Zacatecas, Mexico, and my father - the son of Mexican immigrants - was born near Fresno, California.

Michael Trevino

I grew up in Hollywood, California. A lot of my parents' friends were in the motion picture industry, but I saw their doctor friends as more solid. I admired them; there was a peacefulness in them, a sense of purpose that I liked. So I became very interested in being a surgeon.

Spencer Johnson

I basically left Texas with no money. I was making $3.50 working in some mall, so I didn't have a lot of cash. I took $1,000 and headed to California. Along the way I stopped in Vegas because I had always wanted to see Caesar's Palace. So I stopped there and won $2,500 on a slot machine! It was amazing.

Krista Allen

Everywhere you look, there is a charity or a project in school to get involved in. In eighth grade, there was this program called CJSF, California Junior Scholarship Foundation. We were involved in soup kitchens and toy drives, and your school can set up something like that. If your school doesn't have a program like that, set one up.

Lindsey Shaw

I was born in Orange, California and I grew up in Huntington Beach. I started skateboarding when I was five and continued to do so off and on over the years.

Jason Lee

I want to do feature films. I am flying to Malaysia to be in another feature film. We will be filming that in Malaysia, the Phillipines, and back in California.

Thuy Trang

My family moved from California to New Jersey in the beginning of my sophomore year of high school. I will never forget the first day in a new school, walking into the cafeteria during lunch and not knowing a single soul. I didn't feel confident enough to share a seat at just anyone's table.

Camille Guaty

I have always identified with Joan Didion's depiction of Los Angeles and Southern California, ever since reading 'Play It As It Lays,' 'Slouching Towards Bethlehem' and 'The White Album.'

Henry Rollins

I wouldn't live in California. All that sun makes you sterile.

Alan Alda

All creative people should be required to leave California for three months every year.

Gloria Swanson

Somebody asked my friend Bob Seger, Why do you think the Eagles broke up? He said, Hotel California.

Glenn Frey

California is a tragic country - like Palestine, like every Promised Land.

Christopher Isherwood

Left the ranch in 1883, went to California, going through the States and territories, reached Ogden the latter part of 1883, and San Francisco in 1884.

Calamity Jane

The first treasure California began to surrender after the Gold Rush as the oldest: her land.

John Jakes

California has always led the way on environmental protection and always reaped the benefits, pioneering everything from catalytic convertors on cars to stationary source reduction.

Ed Begley, Jr.

Whatever starts in California unfortunately has an inclination to spread.

Jimmy Carter

California is an unbelievable state.

Drew Barrymore

The law exists for a reason. There is a dominant American culture that people used to want to preserve. That's going by the wayside, too. But if it's now okay for an illegal alien to practice law in California, then can anybody else who's broken the law get a law license? And if not, why not?

Rush Limbaugh

California is a great place to live if you're an orange.

Fred Allen

California is always in my mind.

David Hockney

Besides great climates and lovely beaches, California and Greece share a fondness for dysfunctional politics and feckless budgeting.

James Surowiecki

I'm living in California but I have a place that is mine in Chile and I belong there. I am no longer an exile.

Isabel Allende

California is like an artificial limb the rest of the country doesn't really need. You can quote me on that.

Saul Bellow

I called my business manager in California and said, 'Sell all of my stock' - what little of it I had - and it's the only smart financial move I ever made.

Lauren Bacall

Secretly, I think everyone who makes fun of California really does want to be in California.

Zooey Deschanel

I was a trial lawyer. At the same time, I was a teacher. I taught about the political and social content of film for American University. Then I left and became a teacher at the University of California at Santa Cruz. I taught about the political and social content of film, but I also taught a course in law for undergraduates.

Ben Stein

You know, every family and every business in California

knows what it means to go through tough times.

Carly Fiorina

Arnold Schwarzenegger cut teacher's salaries and parks and libraries rather than raise taxes for the many California millionaires and billionaires.

Adam McKay

When I came to California, it was the mecca of the world. Every young person on the planet wanted to be here.

Joni Mitchell

It kills me when people talk about California hedonism. Anybody who talks about California hedonism has never spent a Christmas in Sacramento.

Joan Didion

The apparent ease of California life is an illusion, and those who believe the illusion real live here in only the most temporary way.

Joan Didion

I like to read Octavia E. Butler's 'Wild Seed' over and over again. And J. California Cooper's 'The Wake of the Wind.' That one makes me cry from joy. I'll mourn - I'll actually mourn - and then I'll cry from joy. She's wonderful.

Jill Scott

If they can't do it in California, it can't be done anywhere.

Taylor Caldwell

When I was growing up, I didn't know there was a world outside of California.

Willie Aames

In actuality, California could be a wonderful place to live. In fact, if you're highly educated and ambitious, you can do quite well here while enjoying the sun and the fun. The only problem: California will then blame you for your success and recommend that all your cash be removed from you.

Ben Shapiro

I grew up in northern California, where it was consistently in the hundreds in the summertime. My dad didn't think he should have to turn on the air conditioning when we had a swimming pool in our backyard; it was our built-in air conditioner.

Summer Sanders

No wonder the film industry started in the desert in California where, like all desert dwellers, they dream their buildings, rather than design them.

Arthur Erickson

For the women in California, they're just downtrodden because they're so gorgeous here. Every hot cheerleader comes to California to make it. The men don't want to get married, they're lazy lions. Matthew McConaughey is their poster boy so they can procreate and live on the beach in the trailer and have kids and have money and be hedonistic.

Patti Stanger

I was born on October 21, 1956 in Burbank, California. My father, Eddie Fisher, was a famous singer. My mother, Debbie Reynolds, was a movie star. Her best-known role was in 'Singin' In The Rain.'

Carrie Fisher

I was an economics major in college, and every summer after school, I would drive my car from California, from Claremont men's college at the time, to New York. And I worked on Wall Street.

Henry Kravis

Move to California. Malibu is paradise.

David Geffen

When President Franklin D. Roosevelt's New Deal eased but did not end the country's economic ills, a trio of leftist radicals - Sen. Huey Long of Louisiana; the Rev. Charles Coughlin, the Detroit radio priest; and Francis Townsend in California - enjoyed temporary notoriety as the spokesmen for nostrums promising more rapid and longer-term cures.

Robert Dallek

I don't want to leave New York and leave my family. I don't like the distance. I just did a movie in California and it's kind of excruciating to be away from them so I think there is that sense.

Sigourney Weaver

During a visit to California, when a friend of my grandmother's told my parents that I must be deaf because I was not responding to sounds, my father was absolutely convinced that I was simply being stubborn.

Marlee Matlin

The ocean-bordered southern part of California has always been a place of Hollywood make-believe, casual opulence, suntans and jewelry.

Dan Jenkins

I came to California and got signed at a young age. And it's not like you see in the movies, where you start rubbing shoulders with Timbaland and Pharrell, and you become a giant pop star.

Bruno Mars

California has a beautiful coastline. It can be a rough coastline. The waves are huge. The rocks are steep. Same thing in Vancouver. It has a beautiful coastline. It's dramatic.

Jennifer Granholm

Hey, I didn't make a big deal out of Hotel California. The 18 million people that bought it did.

Glenn Frey

As one went to Europe to see the living past, so one must visit Southern California to observe the future.

Alison Lurie

I'm from Santa Cruz in Northern California, and the 49ers were my dad and I's bonding time.

Marisa Miller

I like to go for a little drive up the California coast.

Colin Farrell

If I got $300 million from the California Lottery, the first thing I would do is buy the rights to 'Firefly', make it on my own, and distribute it on the Internet.

Nathan Fillion

I'm eternally grateful to the penal system in California for saving my life.

Frank Morgan

I live in California, so I do stand-up paddle board, which is a killer workout. I also run, about four miles every three days.

Ashley Wagner

African-Americans assume I'm named after the notorious Soledad prison or Mount Soledad in California. Latinos want to know if I'm lonely. That doesn't fit, because I grew up with five siblings, and I have four kids of my own, so I'm not lonely at all, though I do often seek solitude, the actual meaning of my name.

Soledad O'Brien

I grew up on the beaches of Southern California surfing and sailing and I've always loved horses so it was part of my dream that I was able to fulfill to have horses.

Bo Derek

In my opinion, Arnold Schwarzenegger wasn't qualified to be governor of California.

James Garner

People look at me, and I dress a little unusually and they think, 'Oh you must be from California.' Of course, people in California think, 'Oh you must be from from Mars,' so, you know, your next-door neighbour is not necessarily the person that you are going to make a connection with.

Howard Rheingold

I heard people saying they were going to become millionaires by the time they were 25 - that's gross and obnoxious, but in California it's looked on as an asset.

Anna Kendrick

On 'Justified,' we're driving all around Southern California trying to find a location that we can call Kentucky.

Timothy Olyphant

Get FREE Kindle Books Every Week, Delivered by Email!

Click Here or Scan the QR Code Below

On PC: http://goo.gl/WYmQvi

www.ingramcontent.com/pod-product-compliance
Lightning Source LLC
Chambersburg PA
CBHW070655290526
45790CB00001B/326